The Jesuits: The History and Legacy of the Catholic Church's Society of Jesus

By Charles River Editors

The Jesuits' emblem

About Charles River Editors

Charles River Editors is a boutique digital publishing company, specializing in bringing history back to life with educational and engaging books on a wide range of topics. Keep up to date with our new and free offerings with this 5 second sign up on our weekly mailing list, and visit Our Kindle Author Page to see other recently published Kindle titles.

We make these books for you and always want to know our readers' opinions, so we encourage you to leave reviews and look forward to publishing new and exciting titles each week.

Introduction

Johann Christoph Handke's fresco depicting the approval of the bylaws of Society of Jesus, with Ignatius of Loyola receiving papal bull Regimini militantis Ecclesiae from Pope Paul III, in the Church of Our Lady Of the Snow in Olomouc

The Jesuits

"Ite, inflammate omnia." ("Go, set the world on fire." – St. Ignatius of Loyola

The Middle Ages remains one of the most defining eras of human civilization. It is an era characterized by illustrious monarchs, valiant knights in shining armor, and magnificent Gothic architecture. It is also an era characterized by fervent friction, brutish barbarism, frequent famines, pestilent plagues, and of course, death. Some say the mortality rate in medieval times was like no other; with about a third of all children dying before the age of 5, it was nearly miraculous for one to live past their 40s.

As a result, medieval people spent their entire lives preparing for the inevitability of death and the afterlife, hoping to one day make their way into the kingdom of Heaven. The Catholic Church did little to alleviate the fear of Hell, a common theme in the sermons delivered by stern priests across Europe. The only surefire way into Heaven, they preached, was for one to pledge their undying love and support to God, with extra points available for the sums and contributions one was willing to gift to the church.

Naturally, the outraged public began to condemn the Catholic Church for its longstanding corruption, and chaos ensued. It was during this period of tempestuous tension that a legendary religious order would emerge.

Of all of the important Catholic men and women who have been venerated over the last 2,000 years, one of the faith's most popular and influential men also lived one of the most unique lives. Like Roman Emperor Constantine the Great, St. Ignatius of Loyola (1491-1556) found God about as far away from church as possible; it was during military service that he underwent a remarkable conversion. A Spanish knight who hailed from a noble Basque family, Ignatius seemed destined for military glory until he was badly wounded in 1521 during the Battle of Pamplona. While convalescing, Ignatius began reading De Vita Christi by Ludolph of Saxony, after which he began a tireless career in service of the Catholic Church.

After spending several years studying the faith, Ignatius formed the Society of Jesus in 1539, and as its Superior General, he sent followers as missionaries across Europe to create schools, colleges, and seminaries. On September 27, 1540, Pope Paul issued a Papal Bull recognizing the church's newest religious order not as the Company of Jesus but as the Society of Jesus. It is still a bit unclear why he chose to change the name. However, there are several possibilities.

First, Pope Paul may have wanted to separate the group, and by extension the Church, from still burning memories of the Crusades. One of the attacks leveled at the Catholic Church by the Protestants was that they had financed the very expensive attempts to reclaim the Holy Land for the Christians by over-taxing the laity, especially through the practice of selling indulgences. It would not do to create a religious order whose name reminded anyone of the Church's checkered military past.

Another reason for the name change may have been Paul III's desired to see the members focus more on theological study and Biblical doctrine than going out into the world to make converts. He was facing threats of serious heresy at home, and had in his midst 10 very intelligent, well-educated men who had all the tools at their disposal to launch a well thought out defense of traditional church teaching. That was what he needed them to focus their energy on.

Finally, he may have seen changing their name as a subtle reminder to Ignatius and the others of who they actually worked for. Even though they had pledged undying loyalty to him and his successors, he was still aware the he lived in a time when many were forgetting their vows and pursuing more appealing doctrines. Better, he may have thought, to make sure everyone knew from the start who was in charge.

The one thing that is clear is that neither Pope Paul, nor Ignatius, ever intended for members of the order to be known as the Jesuits. This term was initially given to them by their critics and was a derogatory term applied to those who spent too much time, in the opinion of those coining the phrase, speaking of Jesus in their conversations. It was only years later that the term became a popular and acceptable nickname for the Society of Jesus, and the Jesuits remain active across the world nearly 500 years later.

The Jesuits: The History and Legacy of the Catholic Church's Society of Jesus examines the life of the group's legendary founder and the order's rise to prominence, its stumbles along the way, as well as the cloud of scandal and conspiracy that continues to hover over the society to this very day. Along with pictures depicting important people, places, and events, you will learn about the Jesuits like never before.

The Jesuits: The History and Legacy of the Catholic Church's Society of Jesus

The Man Behind the Clan

"Act as if everything depended on you; trust as if everything depended on God." – St. Ignatius of Loyola

The Middle Ages, particularly in the West, evokes an enchanting image of glorious kings, comely maidens, and chivalrous knights decked out from head to toe in glinting iron armors, wielding double-edged arming swords. The precious period has gifted remarkable legacies treasured by its future generations. Spectacular collections of captivating cathedrals, colossal castles, and other medieval and Gothic-inspired architecture of the time still stands today. Likewise, modern museums are home to unique paintings, sculptures, illustrated books, and other outlets of creativity crafted in the olden days. The greatest medieval minds had not only penned a new chapter in the arts of literature and philosophy, they introduced the world to mechanical clocks, compasses, gunpowder, spectacles, and farming innovations.

The fact of the matter is these storybook portrayals of the Middle Ages are often highly romanticized, cloaked by a more sinister and dominant element of the period – death. For the majority of the medieval folk, life was grueling, and stricken with calamity, strife, and hardship. After all, there is certainly a reason historians refer to this precarious period as the "Dark Ages."

Due to the abnormally high mortality rates brought about by war, famine, disease, impotent medicine, and ignorance of science, the threat of death constantly loomed over people. Devout Christians lived simple, sinless lives revolving around worship as they prepared for what was to come after death. Religion was such a significant factor in their lives that time was gauged by the annual celebration of saints and martyrs in a system known as the "calendar of saints."

What they longed for was the inevitable, but sweet kiss of "good death." The best case scenario was to die in the cozy comfort of their own bed, encircled by those dearest to their heart. A priest would be present to cleanse them of their sins, guiding them into the light of the afterlife. More than anything, Christians feared "sudden death." This was a tragic and unexpected death that robbed them of the privilege of confessing, and one that would earn them a place in Purgatory, or worse yet, the fiery depths of Hell itself.

The magnitude of death is often reflected in medieval art and literature. One such story is found in the 14th century prayer book "De Lisle Pslater," entitled "The 3 Living and 3 Dead." The somber story tells the tale of a trio of pretentious princes who are visited by a terrifying threesome of worm-infested corpses. The creepy corpses give them a reality check on their mortality, and urge them to live a godly life of piety and charity.

The promises of heaven were commemorated in countless illustrations and paintings. To them, eternal paradise was home to God and His choirs of singing angels, a kingdom bathed in golden light upon the endless sky, surrounded by breathtaking gardens and majestic waterfalls. God is often seen in the center of the heavenly kingdom, perched upon a resplendent throne.

Dante's vision of "Purgatorio" was a cragged mountain with 7 terraces, with the gate to the realm situated on the bottom level, and its peak grazing the clouds of Paradiso. The terraces were categorized by the 7 deadly sins, with the proud souls on the last ring, and the lustful by the peak. Purgatory is the destination for "moderately bad sinners," where they would undergo a purification process before they were allowed to cross the pearly gates.

To the medieval folk, the blazing bowels of eternal damnation was a fate so horrendous, entire lives were dedicated to safeguarding a golden ticket to Heaven. This was a subject so many medieval artists tackled that a term was coined for the beautiful, but morbid artwork – "doom paintings." To these creative minds, Hell was an orgy of suffering and repulsive debauchery. Damned souls guilty of unforgivable "mortal sins" were sodomized and boiled in pots. They were hogtied by frightful demons and force-fed with scorching-hot coals. Scenes of roaring flames, hard labor, ghastly torture, and monstrous humanoid creatures running amok were painted across many a canvas.

The Roman Catholic Church molded all aspects of the medieval lifestyle, as almost all – from the kings to the poorest of peasants – shared the same obsession with the mystery of the afterlife. From an early age, people across the board were injected with the belief that their only path to paradise lay within the church. Every week, from behind every pulpit, priests preached to congregations about the rich rewards of Heaven and the horrors that awaited the sinners in Hell.

Peasants were especially devoted to the Church. Many were sent to work on church-owned lands, and were compensated with paltry to no paychecks at all. Nor were these peasants exempt from required "tithes," which were special taxes paid to the Catholic Church annually, which amounted to about 10 percent of their annual earnings. Most of the time, peasants would have nothing to shell out but seeds, grains, and animals, payment the church gladly accepted. Non-monetary gifts were often hoarded in tithe barns, unattended, and as a result, became inedible and moldy rodent cuisine.

Keeping up with these often crippling tithe payments were crucial to medieval Christians, as many believed this was the literal price to pay for gaining entry into Heaven. Unfortunately, tithes were only one stipulation in the Heaven payment plan. Baptism was not free. Another tax was slapped onto burial plots, which were to be purchased on church land, otherwise known as "holy soil."

As the 15th century came to a close, the Age of Discovery ushered in a new era of marine exploration and globalization. With it came the all the pent-up discontent and furor the public had for the Catholic Church. They thirsted for change. The infuriated public shined the spotlight on the church's blatant corruption. The tax-free entity boasted stunning cathedrals, chapels, and monasteries across the land, which set the tracks of their collision course. The agents of God were living the deluxe lifestyles of the rich and famous, whereas peasants had no choice but to take shelter in "cruck houses," which were squalid and cramped quarters fashioned out of straw, manure, and mud.

The glaring wealth of the church was at its peak in the 16th century. The church began a frenzy of commissioning elaborate, and oftentimes, expensive works of art, such as Michelangelo's masterpiece in the Sistine Chapel. Keep in mind that just one sculpture from Michelangelo cost anywhere between 200 to 450 ducats each (around $5,200 USD to $11,700 USD today). But a certain renovation project propelled by Pope Leo X would have the public in uproar. The pope wanted to reconstruct St. Peter's Basilica, but was short on funding. His Holiness' solution was to reach out to the public, offering indulgences to those who pitched into the construction fees. Indulgences, which had been around since the 13th century, were sums paid to the church in exchange for the absolving of one's sins. Most importantly, it was a guaranteed spot in Heaven's exclusive roster.

Pope Leo X

Apart from this gross abuse of power, popes and priests had become maleficent power-mongers hiding behind the holy cloth. Scandals of these holy men breaking their vows were on the rise. Pope Innocent VIII was a father to a pair of illegitimate children. Gossip mills ran day and night, churning out stories of priests, monks, and nuns engaging in wild, sexual antics.

Moreover, people began to vocalize their contempt for the practice of simony, wherein church positions were sold off to the highest bidders, regardless of their experience. Queues of people lined up to pay both tribute and donations to relics deemed holy by the Catholic Church. The German king, Frederick I, was said to have hosted pilgrimage sites that housed over 17,000 relics. He later allegedly used these profits to fund the construction of German cathedrals and other holy establishments.

It was these abuses that provoked the rise of the Protestant Reformation. A

German professor of theology by the name of Martin Luther sought out to put an end to these perverted practices. It was said that Luther had stumbled upon this epiphany after spending the first half of his life in fear of being excluded from Heaven. He expressed his grievances with the church through a document known as the "95 Theses," criticizing the Catholics' corruption and the idea of "transubstantiation." This was the process of turning bread and wine into the flesh and blood of Christ through the sacrament of the Eucharist.

Luther

The Catholic Church excommunicated Martin Luther along with other leaders of the Reformation, hoping these names would fade into the background. When they could no longer mute the outraged cries of the public, the Catholics regrouped in the 1545 meeting of the Council of Trent. Here, they eliminated the practices of indulgence and simony in an effort to scrub down their tarnished slate, hoping to restore power and order. The "Index of Forbidden Books" was later published, which named and condemned all heretics, including Martin Luther. This battle to reclaim their power is known as the "Counter-Reformation."

Amidst this climate of chaos, an order would emerge with a legacy so unyielding, it not only still exists but continues to thrive today. This bold band of brothers, collectively known as the "Society of Jesus," was fronted by an intrepid and contentious character, St. Ignatius of Loyola. Armed with a vision of their own and a leader whose ambition dwarfed those of his peers, the Jesuits would go where many have dreamed but few have accomplished – taking their operation worldwide. While it is no secret that the Jesuits were among the most powerful and influential religious orders of its time, could there be more to them than meets the eye?

Iñigo Lopez de Oñaz was born on October 23, 1491 in the castle of Loyola. The castle was among the finest constructions in the land, a handsome 5-story castle made of gray stone, adorned with a red roof, and a tower on every corner. Iñigo was the youngest of 13 children in the family, succeeding generations of some of the best warriors that Basque Country has ever known. That said, as distinguished as the family name was, it was one synonymous with crime, deviance, and questionable morals.

Portrait of St. Ignatius of Loyola, by Peter Paul Rubens.

Iñigo knew his mother only through nostalgic anecdotes shared by his siblings, as she had passed on when he was just 7. He would find a second mother in Maria de Garin, the wife of a local blacksmith. Iñigo's father, Don Beltrán de Loyola, was a respected soldier venerated for fighting in the last years of the Reconquista, which was a centuries-long war between the Christians and Muslims, who were battling for the Iberian peninsula. Don, who was also a womanizer that bore children by various different women, would also pass on when Iñigo turned 16.

His grandfather's rap sheet was no better. He, too, was a former soldier often accused of recklessness and criminal activity, such as disturbing the peace in the town of the Guipúzcoan provinces. Eventually, the ticking time bomb of a man had incensed the royal so much that they ordered the destruction of the 2 top stories of the Loyola Castle.

Though Iñigo was of Spanish nobility, he spent his childhood and early teenage years bulking up and training himself as a warrior, showing minimal interest in academics. At the age of his 16, after his father's death, Iñigo landed his first job as a page in court under Juan Velasquez, the treasurer of Castile. Like father, like son, young Iñigo mimicked the patterns instilled into him by the authority figures in his life.

Blessed with dashing good looks, Iñigo was a heartbreaker. Ladies of all ages flocked to him, swooning over his wavy coffee-colored hair and piercing brown eyes. The lady killer was made even more appealing by his athletic build and apparent eye for fashion. Iñigo exploited his charm with his brother, who was his partner-in-crime. Together, they spent the better part of their youth cavorting around town, engaging in steamy, sexual trysts, gambling, and drunken partying.

At this stage of Iñigo's life, most of his siblings had already launched full-fledged careers of their own. Many mourned the death of one of his brothers, who died in a battle across the seas. Another had enlisted in Christopher Columbus' 2nd voyage and was touring around the world. On Iñigo's 18th birthday, he decided it was time to buckle down and start paving the paths of his own future. Thus, he joined the Spanish military in 1509, working under Antonio Manrique de Lara, the 2nd Duke of Nájera and Viceroy of Navarre. While Iñigo soon found himself at home, blending in well with the soldiers and commended for his fighting skills, he was lambasted by his superiors for his bad temper. He was naturally outspoken, but at the same time, sensitive to conflicting opinions, and often challenged those that disagreed with him to impromptu duels. It is said that he once killed a Muslim Moor who questioned the existence of Christ. Iñigo was also described as a cocky, uncouth soldier who often paraded around the base with his cape intentionally left open to show off his dagger and sword.

Despite his lack of proper education, Iñigo had always been fond of a particular type of literature – chivalric romance. One of his all-time favorites was "La Chanson de Roland," or "The Song of Roland," a French epic poem that tells the story of Charlemagne's battle against the Spanish Muslims in the 700s. Another was the "El Cantar de Mio Cid," a poem about Rodrigo Díaz "El Cid" de Vivar, a Castilian nobleman turned beloved war hero.

Throughout Iñigo's years in the military, he would gain one promotion after another, and he soon graduated to "servant of the court." This was a testament to not only the soldier's drive but his tremendous skill in battle. The numerous battles he had entered, he had exited virtually unscathed, wowing his peers and superiors alike. All but one.

In 1521, a massive French army descended upon the fortress town of Pamplona, and the pitiful group of Spanish soldiers stationed in the town was no match for the French. They soon raised their white flags. The surrender of his peers only fired up the determined Iñigo, who refused to back down. He singlehandedly attempted to fend them off on his own and was doing a rather remarkable job until he was struck by a cannonball. The explosion and shrapnel pulverized the bones in his legs. Legend has it the French were so taken by Iñigo's bravery that they hoisted him onto a makeshift stretcher and personally dropped him off at the front steps of the Loyola Castle.

Putting himself back together proved to be an excruciating feat. Iñigo suffered through a series of primitive surgical operations in an age when anesthetics did not yet exist. One of these processes included setting and forcefully breaking the bones of his legs. By the end of it all, Iñigo's legs had become deformed. One of his bones permanently jutted out of his hosiery. With one leg shorter than the other, Iñigo limped for the rest of his life. And just like that, his military career was finished.

During Iñigo's recovery, he took up reading to pass the time. He initially requested for chivalric romances, but ultimately he had to make do with the limited reading material available to him. These were religious works, including an illustrated biography of Christ, as well as a worn-out book about saints. Slowly but surely, Iñigo began to self-reflect, and he eventually found inner peace through his new devotion to Catholicism. When he regained his ability to walk, he traveled to the Spanish town of Montserrat for some soul-searching. There, the changed man supposedly stripped off his fine velvet robes and presented them to a poor man. Later that week, he held an overnight vigil, where he vowed to put his swords and his old life behind him for good.

Iñigo now dreamed of an adventure in the Holy Land, "to kiss the earth where our Lord had walked." In the meantime, he set out on an excursion to the Manresa county of Spain. That excursion turned to a trip that lasted over 10 months. The life Iñigo now lived was a far cry from the comfort and luxuries of nobility. He lodged in of the spare rooms at a local hospital, paying his rent by completing chores around the establishment, and begged around town for sustenance. Every day, Iñigo retired into a faraway cave, where he meditated and prayed to God – at times, up to 7 hours a day.

Iñigo eventually got a ticket on a ship to the Holy Land. He was convinced that he was destined to spend the rest of his days there, converting "infidels" and directing non-believers to the word of God. However, his short-lived campaign was cut short after a few weeks by intervening church authorities. Authorities saw Iñigo as a wild card of a zealot and did not want him stirring up any trouble in an already turbulent region. As such, he was swiftly shipped back home.

Iñigo may have not have been able to carry out his mission in the Holy Land as originally planned, but he had heard his calling. God wanted him to now commit his life to helping others, and the only way to achieve that was the pursuit of higher education. Iñigo, who was already 33, refused to let his age be an issue, so he traveled to Barcelona. There, he attended a free grammar school so that he could be admitted into university. For 2 years, he studied Latin, grammar, literature, and other basic subjects alongside his classmates, who were between the ages of 8 and 14. Once grammar school was behind him, Iñigo traveled to the towns of Alcala and Salamanca, and enrolled in the local universities. A magnet for trouble, he soon garnered another reputation with town authorities, to the extent he was arrested and interrogated at least 3 times for challenging religious leaders. As Iñigo was neither ordained nor a trained theologian, he was charged with the blasphemous spreading of unlicensed theology, which was punishable by law.

It took Iñigo another 3 years before he realized that he was not made for these towns, so he packed up and settled in Paris, where he attended Collège Sainte-Barbe, a branch of the University of Paris. Though he knew a bit of Latin, he was far from fluent, and did not speak much French, but undeterred, he forged on and learned to adjust over time.

Iñigo admired the refreshingly organized system of French schooling. Students operated on a strict routine, with classes starting promptly at 5:00 a.m., and once again after lunch. French students were obligated to complete prerequisites and education levels, which meant that he had to start his education from scratch. First came another round of grammar school, then language and humanities, before he finally graduated to sciences, theology, and philosophy.

After 6 years of studious hard work, Iñigo earned himself a master's degree. His diploma was made out to "Ignatius," an homage to his favorite saint, Ignatius of Antioch. 44-year-old Ignatius would then attempt to pursue a doctorate needed for teaching, but he was rejected due to his age.

A portrait of Ignatius

It was at this university that Ignatius formed a bond with a tight-knit circle of friends. He roomed with Francis Xavier, a Basque nobleman, and Saint Pierre Favre, who hailed from Southern France. That circle slowly expanded with Alfonso Salmeron, a literature and philosophy major; Diego Laynez, a Jewish Spaniard; Nicolaus Bobadilla; and Simão Rodrigues, a wealthy Portuguese student.

Rodrigues

These men were drawn to Ignatius' infectious conviction and his spiritual ambition. What was more, they shared his dream of traveling to the Holy Land, only now, an older and wiser Ignatius devised a back-up plan. If this plan failed a second time, they would head on to Rome and appeal to the pope. There, they would present His Holiness with their vision of mass conversion and the spreading of God's word.

On August 15, 1534, all 7 gathered in the secluded cellar of Saint Denis (now Saint-Pierre de Montmarte), a church on the Monmarmate hill by Paris. A closed ceremony was held, and each companion was inducted into the new organization. These warriors of Christ christened themselves the Company of Jesus, or "Amigos en El Señor" – "Friends in the Lord."

Saint-Pierre de Montmarte

The Mechanics of the Order

"I have studied at Barcelona, at Salamanca, at Alcala, at Paris; what have I learned? The language of doubt; but in me there was no harbor for doubt. Jesus came, and my trust in God has grown by the doubts of men." – St. Ignatius of Loyola

The original vision of the order was set down in a formal charter known as the "Formula of the Institute." Ignatius was on the hunt for a "soldier of God" who was searching for purpose in his life. The choice candidate was a man, married or unmarried, who was willing to give his life up to the Lord. If chosen, these candidates would be required to take solemn, unbreakable vows of "perpetual chastity, poverty, and obedience."

On top of those qualities, candidates would be of strong character and moral backbone, and they would possessethe humility and the wherewithal to reconcile with those who have wronged them in the past. Active listening skills and the capacity to remain unbiased were other important attributes necessary to take part in the order, as these candidates would one day be tasked with hearing confessions and performing other sacramental rites. These were candidates who had to be prepared to live a simple life, free of material pleasures, as they would now live among the poor. Candidates were to accept that they would have no other obligations in life but to preach the word of God, near or far. Altruism was yet another crucial quality, as candidates had to prepare themselves to serve the less fortunate. This included nursing and providing comfort to prisoners and hospital patients, and other charitable deeds.

These soldiers of God had one chief mission – to defend and spread the word about the Roman Catholic faith to people of all ages, but above all, to children, freethinkers, and "unlettered persons in Christianity."

Back in 1533, before the companions had even convened for their first meeting, Ignatius had already drafted the order's constitution. His central principle would later become the Jesuits' unofficial motto: "Ad Maoirem Dei Gloriam," which translates to "for the greater glory of God." The Society of Jesus would later be registered as a "mendicant" order, meaning this non-profit organization relied on alms and donations from supporters and benefactors.

Ignatius's finalized rules were fairly simple. First and foremost, he reiterated the significance of the 3 solemn vows, as well as another of servitude to the pope, which was to be taken when the Jesuit was selected for a mission. There was no requirement to attend regular Masses or communal prayers, but meditation was a must. Missionaries could move at their own pace, as long as the word of God was being preached. They were also never to accept the position of bishop without the pope's blessing. Fasting, or any other acts of mortification, which was the intentional subduing of natural bodily desires) were not to be approved without a proper medical report.

There was no Jesuit uniform, but a dress code had to be adhered to. Members were to dress "properly" and choose only the most basic of fashion choices, conforming to the social standards of their residence. In Ignatius' day, they wore special cassocks; these were black or dark robes tied around the waist with a matching cincture (a sash). Some wore a "biretta," which was a square hat with 4 peaks that joined together on its crown, topped off with a round, fluffy "tuft." Those in the higher classes of the order might also choose to wear a cape.

A depiction of Ignatius

A 17th century depiction of Jesuits in India

Ignatius and his companions would spend the first year or two jotting down itineraries for the sacred space of the Middle East, only to crumple them up and toss them up aside with disgruntled grunts each time. By their third year, a conflict between Charles V, King of Spain and the Holy Roman Emperor, and King Francis I of France had bubbled over and spilled into war. The bitter kings had at been at each other's throats over territories in Northern Italy, predominantly the Duchy of Milan. The duchy was an Italian state that had been claimed by the Holy Roman Empire since the late 14th century. With the swarms of French and Spanish troops at the borders, Ignatius knew it was time to put their wishful journey to the Holy Lands to rest.

Charles V

In 1537, the Friends in the Lord set a new plan into motion. Bearing the Formula of the Institute, the 7 men trekked to Vatican City, where they arranged a special meeting with Pope Paul III. There, a beaming but anxious Ignatius presented his charter, outlining his aspiring order's candidacy requirements, their objectives, their dedication to missionary work, and their vow to pledge allegiance to His Holiness.

Pope Paul III

On their way to see the pope, Ignatius and his companions had made a pit stop at La Storta, and turned in for the night. The next morning, Ignatius claimed that God and Jesus had come to him in a vision. Jesus had allegedly said to him, "I want you to serve us." God would also warn him about the difficulties they might happen upon in Rome. This dream only fueled Ignatius's burning determination.

The pope was thrilled with their initiative, as the continent had, in his opinion, reached the peak of paganism and anti-Catholic heresy. Missionary work would be the perfect plan to revive the interest in Catholicism. More so, the founder's military background was a plus, as he should possess the discipline required to carry out such a mission. Best of all, the pope would now have his own personal religious army of sorts at his disposal. And so, Pope Paul III showered Ignatius and his companions with accolades. On the 24th of June that year, all 7 were ordained by the Bishop of Arbe.

The 7 were now ordained and officially endorsed by the pope, but it would take several months before the board of cardinals finally ratified the order's constitution. On September 27, 1540, Pope Paul III recognized the order through a papal bull called the "Regimini militantis ecclesiae," on condition that the order accept no more than 60 members. 10 years later, the succeeding pope, Julius III, removed that limit with a second bull entitled " Exposcit debitum."

Pope Julius III

In April of 1541, Ignatius was elected as the first Superior General, or the "Praepositus Generalis," the title awarded to the head of the order. Later that year, the following re-branded themselves as the "Society of Jesus." The term "Jesuit" was first applied to the followers of the order as a derogatory term and was never used by Ignatius or his first batch of companions, but later members would embrace the term.

The Superior General, or as some prefer to be called, the "Father General," is elected by the entire congregation. It is an honorable position one is expected to hold until death, or in some rare cases, resignation. Superior Generals, who hold absolute authority over the enterprise, are required to be formally authorized and championed by the pope.

A cabinet of assistants was formed to aid Ignatius as Superior General.

These assistants would act as an inner council and his right-hand men, known as the "Curia." 4 were designated as "assistants for provident care," and another secretary appointed to transcribe records and organize the daily operations. There was an "admonitor," which was essentially a spy who drew up confidential reports about problematic members and issues within the community. Other cabinet members were regional assistants who were responsible for overseeing a certain region or ministry.

The brotherhood of priests was split into various provinces, with a "Provincial Superior," otherwise known as simply "General," or "Provincial," to head each section. Provincial Superiors had authority over all the Jesuits and ministries in his provinces. Each was advised by a secretary known as a "Socius." Novice masters, or "Rectors," were those that ran the daily operations within the provinces. All staff elected under the Provincial Superiors were nominated by them, but had to be approved by other Provincials, as well as the Superior General.

There were 4 classes in Ignatius' order. Freshly accepted candidates were known as "Novices." These were trainees taking the order out for a test drive, living among the taxing training and discipline provided by the order. After 2 years, those who wished to remain in the brotherhood graduated to the stage of "Formed Scholastics." Those at this stage were ordained into the priesthood and required to take simple vows, remaining under scrutiny by his superiors from anywhere between 2 to 15 years. Traditionally, in their third year as Formed Scholastics, Jesuits would go through a probationary period. Superiors assessed their performance and identified the talents unique to these members.

The third class was the "Formed Coadjutors." At this juncture, these members would have completed all required ecclesiastical courses and training. These members took on a more serious set of vows. The order was now bound to these Formed Coadjutors, a bond that would only be broken if an unpardonable act of treachery or offense was committed.

The elite of the Jesuits lay in the final class – the "Professed." These select priests were required to not only take the 3 solemn vows but also another oath of obedience and a lifetime of servitude to the pope. The Professed were to do the pope's bidding without questioning him, and must not only wholeheartedly accept but go far and beyond with missions they were tasked with.

The first candidates were mostly religious and doctoral students from European schools and universities, namely post-graduate students. Small business owners with a zest for faith, as well as priests of similar fellowships were also reeled in by the order. Provincials examined each candidate personally. Only with his approval would the aspiring Jesuit be presented to 4 other Provincials or superiors, who decided whether or not the candidate would be admitted into the brotherhood.

Candidates underwent thorough background checks and were grilled about their pasts, from their parents' names to how much debt they owed. Those with repeat criminal histories, or showed signs of any "mental instability," were turned away. Candidates with a past of flitting from one organization to another were also rejected, as this indicated the candidate's lack of follow-through.

Members of this order lived a life shaped by routine. Every morning, they rose at the break of daylight and made a beeline for the chapel, where they meditated on a subject they had chosen the night prior. After breakfast, members ticked off their chores for the day, mainly manual labor and charitable deeds outside the community. In their spare time, they studied books about Catholic history and famous missionaries.

To test their vocation, members-in-training were entrusted with leading classes of their own in small village churches. To test their modesty and perseverance, they were sent on pilgrimages without money, and at times, sent out to the streets for weeks to live the life of a pauper. To test their patience, generosity, and willingness for self-sacrifice, they were sent to notorious jailhouses and disease-ridden hospitals to cater to the helpless and needy.

The life of a Jesuit was not, and is not, for the weak-minded.

A Philosophy is Born

An 18th century depiction of a Jesuit missionary

"Remember that the good angels do what they can to preserve men from sin and obtain God's honor. But they do not lose courage when men fail." – St.

Ignatius of Loyola

The goal of the order's first campaign around Europe was to establish Jesuit-approved schools across the continent, making their presence known. There, Jesuits who were properly trained in classical studies and theology were tasked with passing on the knowledge to students, for either a minimal fee, but ideally, no charge at all. These Jesuits were also part-time scribes, who produced books, articles, and pamphlets that promoted the Jesuit movement.

A separate set of brothers would evangelize non-Christians and "barbarians" along the way, as well as defend the sacrament of the Holy Communion, a movement that would later expand across the borders. Ignatius' primary target for mass conversion were the Muslims, as this was when Islam had begun to spread across Europe. That attention would later shift to the Protestants.

As highly as Ignatius revered the Catholic Church, it was common knowledge that it was in desperate need of reform. One of the biggest downfalls of the church, he believed, was its lack of infrastructure when it came to educating the public. With the new Jesuit institutions set in place, he hoped to help resolve that problem. Another downfall was the decay of corruption, which was running rampant within the church. One of the oaths taken by Jesuits was to forever reject simony and other forms of bribery, as dishonesty and greed had no place in their philosophy.

According to Ignatius and his companions, the first step to achieving true reform was a total cleansing and spiritual awakening of the individual. As Ignatius himself put it, "He who goes about to reform the world must begin with himself, or he loses his labor." The practice of retreats, known as "Spiritual Exercises," was established. The distinctive Jesuit creation of self-meditation consisted of a month-long period of absolute silence, solitude, and reflection on Christ, as well as themselves.

After this spell of solitude, Jesuits engaged in another "retreat in daily life." They were assigned Spiritual Directors that they were to shadow. They tagged along on prayer sessions, and also met regularly with their directors for another month. In these meetings, Jesuits could discuss their advancement in the order, as well as consult their directors about any visions or messages that may have appeared to them during these retreats.

Ignatius created a guideline for these exercises, complete with milestones, prayers, and a detailed how-to on meditation and reinforcing one's relationship with God. "Spirits," both good and evil, were are to influence one's decision making. Good spirits bring love, joy, and peace, and at times, necessary sadness and desolation, which was required to better themselves. On the other end of the spectrum, evil spirits invite anger, doubt, confusion, and stubbornness, elements that hinder change. These exercises, which promote "discernment," are designed to tell these spirits apart.

The first week of the solitary retreat is called "Purgation." At this stage, the Jesuit identifies "global" and "personal" sin, and evaluates their fears, guilt, lack of confidence, and other shortcomings. They are introduced to Christ once again, and they explore the significance of their Savior's sacrifice. They contemplate what it means to be a disciple of Christ, and accept what it means to submit their lives to God.

By the second week, a Jesuit enters the stage of "Illumination." Here, he gains a deeper understanding of Christ's motives and messages. He must understand and accept that following Christ through thick and thin is a choice. He makes an internal vow to reject evil, greed, and other material desires for the rest of his life, with only God and the mission of the Jesuits at heart.

The final 2 weeks are known as the "Union." By the end of the retreat, Jesuits should have summoned the strength within to carry out the mission. They are now reformed individuals, equipped with a deeper understanding of compassion and humility, and would emerge with nothing but love and peace in their hearts.

Later, in 1599, an international team of Jesuit scholars created the "Ratio Studiorum," which outlined the Jesuit education system. The document contained regulations for all Jesuit officials and teachers and listed all the approved courses, mainly philosophy, theology, classical literature, poetry, as well as the foreign languages of Latin and Greek. The document was once again revised in 1832, which saw the subjects of natural sciences, mathematics, general history, and geography added to the curriculum.

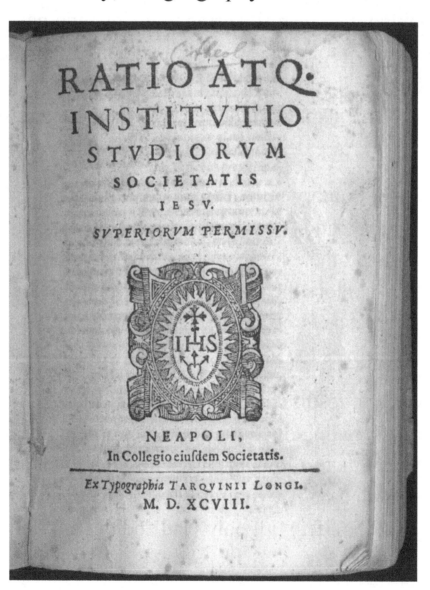

A 16th century version of the Ratio Studiorum

While the order, like many brotherhoods, is known for its all-male membership, that has not always been the case. As claimed by nonfiction writer, Rogelio Garcia-Mateo: "The Society [of Jesus] owes its existence to many women." Of the 7,000 letters authored by Ignatius as Superior General, at least 100 of them had been addressed to women. The first women were said to have approached Ignatius in Manresa, where he was composing the Spiritual Exercises. These women, all friends, were Hieronima Claver, who operated a hospital for the needy in Santa Lucia; Iñes Pascual, a wealthy widow; and Isabel Roser, his biggest, and perhaps most rabid fan. The pope permitted all 3 women to follow Ignatius, and a temporary female branch was established in 1545.

Women, many of them widowed, approached Ignatius and his companions. They were eager to promote the Jesuit vision, but many refused to be "cloistered nuns." This would later pose problems, which stemmed from a lack of management within the women's branch.

Historians cannot seem to agree on what it was that made the order close its doors to women. Some say the answer lay with his most loyal follower, Isabel. Ignatius had once praised her in a letter, telling her "for to you I owe more than anyone in my life." That affection, however, would soon change. The increasingly demanding Isabel became difficult to work with. She latched onto him like a leech for spiritual guidance, so much so that her overbearing requests began to disrupt the flow of daily operations. In turn, Ignatius turned to the pope and asked him to eliminate Isabel's Jesuit vows. That same year, in 1547, women were banned from entering the order altogether.

Another notable and alleged member that may have played a part in the eradication of the women's branch was 19-year-old Joanna of Austria, the Princess of Portugal and the daughter of Charles V. Joanna, too, became a widow when her husband, João Manuel, Prince and former heir to the Portuguese throne, died of tuberculosis in 1554. Around this time, Joanna became an avid supporter of the Jesuits, and made hefty donations to the order on a regular basis.

Joanna

A year after her husband's death, Joanna entered the order and accepted all 3 of the Jesuit vows. This meant she could never remarry, which would derail her father's plans. Charles had hoped to someday pair her off with another royal powerhouse, so he could potentially create future alliances with other nations.

Rather than risk the king's wrath, Ignatius urged Joanna to keep her vows a secret. This way, she could still live the life of a Jesuit, but no one would be any the wiser. Joanna's name is never mentioned in the Jesuit archives, but some historians believe she had assumed the pseudonym of either "Mateo

Sanches" or "Montoya." In accordance with her vows, she remained single for the rest of her life. Some suggest that it had been the princess' interference, as well as her attempt to control Ignatius and other superiors, that turned the Jesuits off to the idea of women in their order completely.

Jesuits Without Borders

A depiction of a Jesuit in China

A depiction of Jesuit Père Marquette and Native Americans

"Teach us to give, and not to count the cost." – St. Ignatius of Loyola

Besides establishing schools and the constant preaching of Spiritual Exercises, the order was an active aid to all communities. One of their more memorable acts of community service was spearheaded by Ignatius himself. A program was initially set in place for runaway women and former prostitutes, which would help relocate the women in secluded convents. Nonetheless, non-Christian women were put off by their re-housing destinations, so Ignatius was left with no choice but to come up with another plan. He scrounged up donations, some from the church, but mostly from affluent noblewomen, and created the St. Martha's House in 1543.

St. Martha's House became a safe haven for young girls and women who had nowhere to go. As more noblewomen learned about the project, the donations began to pour in. Among these were the Jesuit admirers, Joanna of Castile and Leonor Osorio. The latter was said to have welcomed 16 prostitutes into her home and helped restart their lives. By the end of its first year, 80 women were living in St. Martha's. Similar institutions later popped up in more Italian and Spanish cities.

Ignatius gained many female supporters through the establishment of St. Martha's House, as well as his history of charitable acts aimed at women. Back in 1539, Faustina de Jancolini, a Roman widow, donated her house and several plots of land to Ignatius and the Jesuits. An Austrian noblewoman handed over 300 ducats (approximately $7,800 USD today), which was to be used to provide food and shelter for the penniless. In 1554, another noblewoman, Donna Maria Frassoni, would make another whopping donation of 70,000 scudi (over $300,000 USD) to construct a Jesuit church and university in the Italian city of Ferrara.

Other Jesuits who worked outside of the education program were snatched up by the pope and sent to Germany, where they were to debate Catholic critics. Among these German-bound missionaries was Favre, one of the original 7 companions. Through his effortless charm, dedication to preaching, and his slick debate skills, he helped reawaken Catholicism in Germany. Other original companions, such as Salmeron and Laynez, were sent to the Council of Trent as "papal theologians."

At first, the creation of Jesuit schools worldwide was a vision Ignatius and early Jesuits had trouble grasping. They had visualized themselves as independent missionaries, sent across the seas for months a time. For a while, Ignatius fought for the missionary method of preaching. Running a network of schools was a tough business they intended to dabble in, rather than specialize.

Ignatius would only see the value in schools when another Jesuit, Claude Jay, convinced him that the only way to escape the probing eyes of German authorities was to create their own school in Germany. Ignatius soon warmed up to the idea. He solidified agreements with local authorities, who would cough up the funding for Jesuit schools, so that free education could be within reach to even the most impoverished of the masses.

The steady, and at times, explosive expansion of the order would exceed Ignatius' expectations with flying colors. In early 1537, when Ignatius and his companions were newly ordained, the Jesuit hosted a measly 10 followers. By the time of Ignatius' death from malaria in 1556, the order had founded 74 colleges stretched across 3 different continents – Japan, Brazil, and Congo, with a membership of at least 1,000 worldwide.

Francis Xavier, yet another one of the original 7, is often credited with kick-starting the Jesuit movement in Asia. While stationed in Japan, Xavier not only befriended the locals, he studied and learned to speak the basics of the foreign language. In the beginning of his journey, his attempts at spreading the word in Japan were met by several roadblocks in the form of unswerving Japanese authorities until he was finally given a chance to preach in Yamaguchi. On his 35th birthday, the pope appointed him the "Apostolic Nuncio to the East."

Xavier

During Xavier's stay in Japan, he was said to have succeeded in the conversion of at least a few hundred Japanese people. The Jesuits eventually developed a presence in Japan that was so strong, they were granted "feudal fiefdom" of the Nagasaki prefecture in 1580. This gave them full authority over the Nagasaki territory. 7 years later, Japanese authorities revoked their title, as they began to grow wary over the skyrocketing number of Catholics in their country.

Xavier would also spend some time in Indonesia and the Portuguese Moluccas, and planned to take the movement to China, often gushing about the colorful culture. He ultimately settled in Goa of then Portuguese-owned

India, in 1541. There, he noticed the surplus of churches and the stark lack of educators, and diverted his attention to remedying the problem.

For his first 5 months there, Xavier evangelized and tended to the sick in hospitals. After his rounds, he strolled out into the city streets, armed with a bell and a bible. At the jingle of his bell, homeless children herded towards him. Day after day, Xavier fed them and taught them about the Lord. In 1542, he became the dean of the St. Paul's College in Goa, the first Jesuit headquarters in Asia. Unfortunately, Xavier died at age 46 a decade later, and never fulfilled his dream of exploring the precious jewel of the East.

In the next 200 years following Ignatius' passing, the Society of Jesus experienced a phenomenal growth spurt. More and more Jesuits continued to operate inner-city churches and carried on their quest for worldwide evangelization. Jesuits began to assign missions of their own to their underlings. Retreat houses sprung up all across the globe. The order pursued even more progressive projects, which attracted the attention of royals and authorities from all 4 corners of the world. They were now the private confessors to kings and queens. More praises were sung when Jesuit priests began to make groundbreaking strides in the literature of translation.

Jesuits abroad worked day and night to translate ecclesiastical and classical works. One such work is the Nippo Jisho, otherwise known as the "Japanese-Portuguese Dictionary," compiled by a collection of Jesuit priests in 1603. Jesuits who had posted up in various indigenous regions in Europe and America would also devote time and effort to learning their native languages.

Some Jesuits formed guilds and confraternities under the name of the order. In 1563, a Belgian Jesuit, Jan Leunis, founded the Sodality of Our Lady, which "aims at fostering in its members an ardent devotion, reverence, and filial love towards the Blessed Virgin Mary." At the outset, the school was open only to young boys, but dozens of sodalities were later developed in different European cities for students, priests, artisans, and other professionals.

By the year 1600, 245 Jesuit schools and establishments were in operation. Just 15 years later, that number swelled to 372. This had gone far past sheer beginner's luck. The order was on a hot streak, and they were only just warming up.

Xavier was never afforded a chance of wrapping his fingers around his holy grail, but the following generation of his brethren would bring his dream to fruition. In 1594, a party of priests, led by Matteo Ricci, made Jesuit history as they hitched their ship to the post of the Macanese dock. The Jesuits rolled up their sleeves and went to work, evangelizing the Macanese people, setting up charity programs for the poor, and building Jesuit schools, such as the St. Paul's College of Macau.

This was a time when Chinese interest in Western sciences and astronomy were at an all-time high. Bearing this in mind, the Jesuits pounced on the opportunity. They translated mathematical and scientific works from the West into Chinese to entice Chinese scholars and influential figures. Jesuits and Chinese intellects collaborated to map out the skies, producing the world's first modern celestial cartography.

Confucian works were also translated into a variety of European languages. This fusion of Jesuit and Confucian philosophy resulted in the Chinese Rites Controversy during the 17th and 18th centuries. Ricci and his companions were accused of creating a "Chinese" version of the church, which utilized Confucian principles and rituals that the Roman Catholic Church blasted as idolatrous. Soon after, the Jesuits were expelled from China.

A separate band of Jesuits made more breakthroughs in North America during the 1600s. Jesuits in Quebec, Canada, mingled with the native tribes, learning their customs, and "redeeming" the Native Americans. In 1626, a French Jesuit priest, Jean de Brébeuf, who lived among the Huron tribe, wrote the first Native American-European translation dictionary. By 1639, it was decided that a proper headquarters was needed for Jesuit missionaries in Huronia.

A town was built for the Jesuit purpose, one of many, named "Sainte-Marie." The Jesuits invited the natives to live among them in these enclaves (or as the Jesuits called them, "reductions"), and soon gained the respect of the natives for the missionaries' willingness to embrace their customs. Though it proved difficult to convert the natives, both parties lived in harmony.

Pierre-Jean De Smet, a Belgian Jesuit, was said to have covered one of the widest ranges throughout his missionary career, totaling over 180,000 miles. He, too, worked with the natives in the Midwest of the United States in the 19th century. Smet would also earn himself the nickname of "Sitting Bull" after he triumphantly arranged a meeting between a Sioux war chief and the American government.

De Smet

Meanwhile, other Jesuits had scattered across South America. The first assemblage arrived in the Vice-royalty of Peru, also home to an assortment of indigenous peoples. José de Acosta, one of the Jesuit leaders, had planned on infiltrating the tribes, but while the Viceroy of Peru encouraged this, Acosta was asked to put the natives in charge of their own parishes, an idea he promptly rejected. Instead, Acosta and his men steered their attention towards the Peruvian elite.

Another noteworthy name was Jesuit Alfonso de Sandoval, based in Cartagena, Colombia. Sandoval developed his own operation to evangelize slaves, an account he has memorialized in his autobiographies. Accompanied by an assistant, he ducked into a slave ship parked by the port. He roamed through rows upon rows of shackled, shivering slaves, feeding them water and scraps of food. As he fed them, he attempted to convert them, but to little avail, presumably because the slaves had more pressing things on their minds.

In the years that followed, the Jesuits planted flags in a slew of other locations, including Ethiopia, Colonial Brazil, Paraguay, Mexico, the Philippines, and many more others. The Society of Jesus had become a true force to be reckoned with. Naturally, the number of Jesuit supporters steadily climbed – but so did their detractors.

Suppression

"[T]heir [the Jesuit Church] restoration...is indeed a step towards darkness, cruelty, despotism...and death." – John Adams, 2nd President of the United States

The Jesuits have never been a stranger to conflict, and Ignatius himself had come across his fair share of critics. Many may have praised him for the innovations he brought forth with his Spiritual Exercises, yet many of the top clergymen of the Catholic Church disapproved, censuring his concepts as "foreign" and "unorthodox." Some of them went so far as to accuse the order of secretly working with the Bavarian Illuminati, as well as other socially unaccepted brotherhoods. These accusations became a common theme that echoed across the Jesuit communities around the world.

Others began to vilify the Jesuits as dangerously liberal free-thinkers, as the order often found themselves leaning towards the left of the political spectrum when it came to heated Catholic debates. The generations of Jesuits that succeeded Ignatius and his companions not only condoned, but encouraged the toleration of other religions. Their advocacy of free education, coupled with their focus on living a life of poverty, led to gossip about their underlying Socialist motives.

Jesuit ideology would later lead to their persecution. The anticlerical Adolf

Hitler despised the Roman Catholic Church, and he harbored a special resentment for the Jesuits. Brothers of the order were swept up by the Gestapo and thrown into persecution camps.

At times, it appeared as if the order's optimism clouded their judgment. Most Jesuit missions managed to live peacefully alongside the natives for decades, but this was not always the case. One of their more daunting errors was the failed mission in Florida during the late 1500s.

Juan Rogel, who was among the first to settle in Florida, raved about what seemed to have been the mission's promising start. In a letter addressed to his superiors back home, he claimed that Florida was "ready for a spiritual harvest." Unbeknownst to Rogel, converting the natives would be nowhere as easy as he had hoped. For months, they suffered violent ambushes by the natives who wanted them off their land. 2 years later, Florida-based Jesuits asked to be pulled out of the territory. Said a Jesuit in an impassioned harangue about the failed mission, "[The natives] are sensual, savage beasts who preferred going to hell with the devil than to heaven with the Christians."

With the order growing at an exponential rate, criticism and disagreement were inescapable, but as the order approached the 17th century, they would experience a wave of tumult unlike any other before. The Republic of Venice had never been the papacy's biggest supporter, with both ends often bickering over jurisdictional matters, but by 1602, their rickety bridge of relations began to crumble. Venetian authorities established a series of laws targeted on the Church known as the Venetian Interdicts. Church-owned lands were confiscated by the dozen. The next year, the government restricted the building of churches by banning construction without the state's permission. This soon led to the expulsion of several religious orders, including the Jesuits.

By the mid-18th century, the Jesuit's critics multiplied, condemning them for "political maneuvering" and exercising manipulative tactics to squeeze through loopholes that allowed them to control the government and its people. At this point, there were more than 22,000 registered Jesuits running 700 colleges and 200 seminaries around the world. Monarchs in European countries were displeased by the overwhelming support they attracted, as well as their connections with various powerful benefactors. Worse yet, Jesuit books were now among the most widely circulated worldwide, tainting the impressionable minds of the public with their toxic ideas. Authorities across Europe seemed to come to a concurrent, but unspoken agreement – the Jesuits had to be stopped.

As Europe entered the Enlightenment Era in the 1700s, the appeal of the Catholic Church and its antiquated, "superstitious" ideas began to wane. The Society of Jesus, which worked hand-in-hand with the papacy, got lumped into the category of outdated powers many wanted extinct. Slowly, rumors about the Jesuits, many of them unfounded, began to spread. One of the most sensational rumors was that the deceptive Jesuits were secret agents working for the pope who hoped to control the world through the vehicle of Catholicism. This would soon lead to what is now known as the infamous Jesuit Suppression.

Operating Jesuit schools on donations had always been a questionable business model, but then again, profit has always placed last on the Jesuit agenda. Some Jesuit missionaries began to toy with the trading business, most notably in China, Japan, and the Caribbean. Many of these missionaries proved to be quite capable with their new side projects, which furrowed the brows of businessmen and authorities alike. The only problem was, Jesuit-owned businesses were prohibited by canon law.

The trouble began in Portugal. Relations between the Jesuits and Portuguese worsened when Sebastião de Carvalho, Count of Oeiras was appointed minister of state by King Joseph I of Portugal. Carvalho promoted a brand of "extreme regalism," fighting for the sovereign's control over ecclesiastical issues. Tensions escalated when Carvalho and the Jesuits engaged in a territorial dispute over the city of Colonia del Sacramento in Uruguay.

Sebastião de Carvalho

It would not be long before Carvalho's supporters began to badmouth the Jesuits. The order was accused of partaking in "illicit, public, and scandalous commerce." Carvalho eventually convinced the pope to assign Portuguese cardinal, Francisco de Saldanha, to look into these accusations.

Shortly after, Portuguese Jesuits became the subject of an even graver accusation following the assassination attempt on King Joseph I in September of 1758. Several Jesuits were rounded up and accused of educating the conspirator, Jean Châtel. In January of 1759, Carvalho issued a decree to confiscate all property and assets of the Portuguese Jesuit society. About a thousand of these Jesuits were deported. Others were arrested and executed, and the Jesuits were officially banned from Portugal.

Perhaps the most pivotal factor that contributed to the Jesuit suppression was Antoine de la Valette, who had been named Superior General of all French Jesuit bases in Central and South America in 1754. Valette was one of the first of the Jesuit entrepreneurs, whose overambitious trading empire met its unwitting demise when it incurred a debilitating debt of 2.4 million lires (about $10.4 million USD). Before the debts could be settled, the case was tried in court, and the whole of the French Jesuit society was rendered responsible for the unpaid fees.

When the French society failed to meet payment deadlines, all their assets were seized. The order was officially abolished in November of 1764. What followed was a domino-effect of falling societies. Spain issued a similar ban on Jesuits in 1767. 3 years later, Austria followed suit.

Pope Clement XIII himself, once a staunch defender of the Jesuits, issued a papal bull that banned the order in July 21, 1773. This bull went into effect in all countries at once, barring Russia and the Kingdom of Prussia. Luckily for the Jesuits, millions of Catholics lived in Polish provinces, which were in Prussia's possession at the time, so not all hope was lost for the movement. Eventually, Pope Pius VII canceled the papal bull and restored the order in August of 1814.

Pope Clement III

Pope Pius VII

Though the Jesuits have often been criticized for being overly liberal, President John Adams and a number of other American presidents remained suspicious of the order. Many of them openly voiced their disappointment about the restoration of the Society of Jesus. In a letter addressed to Thomas Jefferson in May 1816, Adams wrote, "I do not like the reappearance of the Jesuits...[they wear] many disguises as only a king of the gypsies can assume, dressed as printers, publishers, and schoolmasters. If there was ever a man who merited more damnation on earth and in Hell, it is this society of Loyola's." Jefferson was said to have written back to his predecessor, "Like you, I disapprove of the restoration of the Jesuits, for it means a step backwards from light into darkness."

The Jesuit Legacy

"If our church is not marked by caring for the poor, the oppressed, the hungry, we are guilty of heresy." – St. Ignatius of Loyola

Whether or not one agrees with Jesuit principles, the headway their contributions have made in the advancement of arts and sciences is commendable. As a matter of fact, the Jesuits' influence on science is so prominent that the order was described as "the single most important contributor to experimental physics in the 17th century." The greatest scholars in the world would soon hunt them down for their exemplary educational backgrounds and expertise in an array of scientific fields.

For one, seismology, the scientific study of earthquakes and similar planetary waves, is often referred to by modern scientists as the "Jesuit science." From the 16th-18th centuries, Jesuit scientists in the United States were some of the first to analyze single earthquakes and their causes. Research stations dedicated to the study of the science were established by Jesuits around the world. In 1909, the Jesuit Seismological Association was founded, which became the first network of seismological stations in history, connecting scientists from all over the United States. More seismological stations would later pop up in Asia, Africa, and South America.

By the 18th century, Jesuit scientists worldwide were making their marks in their own specific fields, contributing to dozens of modern inventions. Jesuits interested in horology helped develop clocks, barometers, and pantographs. German Jesuit and famed astronomer, Christopher Clavius, created the "Gregorian" calendar, which is still the most commonly used calendar today, particularly in the West. In 1671, another German Jesuit, Athanasius Kircher, was credited with making pioneering discoveries in bacteriology. His work would later be referenced in the "germ theory of disease."

Astronomy mavens were another integral component to the Jesuit-led scientific advancement. Not only did they help better telescopes and microscopes, Jesuits of this era were also said to have been the first to identify Saturn's rings, as well as the "colored bands" on Jupiter's surface, and the breathtaking nebula of the Andromeda Galaxy. By 1750, 30 of the world's 130 astronomical observatories were operated by Jesuits.

On top of the order's leading-edge achievements on celestial cartography in China, Jesuit scientists also helped develop several mathematical theories and tried their hands at other sciences, which included minting the division of time zones in the country. Jesuits in China were also at the forefront of exploration. They are said to have helped establish the Russo-Chinese border, and have also allegedly chanced upon a then-undiscovered land route that ran between China and India. Other Jesuit explorers discovered at least 5 of the world's most famous rivers, including the Missouri.

Among one of the most impactful of the scientific leaps in China was Matteo Ricci's "Black Tulip" map. Previous Chinese-made maps only showed 15 of the Chinese provinces, but Ricci's exquisitely detailed version included the Americas. Some historians maintain that the "Black Tulip" is even more detailed than most contemporary hand-drawn maps today.

Ming Dynasty scholars were supposedly one of the Jesuit's steadfast admirers, with the order earning the scholars' respect through their "impressive...knowledge of astronomy, calendar-making, mathematics, hydraulics, and geography."

Along with the hundreds of Jesuit colleges, universities, seminaries, and non-profit charities around the globe, a number of Jesuits have also been recognized for taking their undying devotion of the cause to the next level.

Martin Gilbert, a Jewish historian, among many others, celebrates the Jesuits' involvement in the rescue operation for the Jews during the Holocaust in numerous books, articles, and essays. At least 14 Jesuit priests were said to have taken in hundreds of Jewish children, storing them in the basements and cellars of schools and monasteries whenever the Gestapo came into town. A plaque that salutes 152 Jesuit priests for their rescue efforts in the Holocaust still stands in the Jesuit Rockhurst University in Missouri.

Among these noble souls is a medley of names many Jesuits today honor as martyrs. One of these names was Jean de Brébeuf. In 1625, Brébeuf's superiors, who marveled at his extraordinary language skills, sent him on a mission to Huronia. 9 years later, there was a lethal outbreak of smallpox and dysentery among the native tribes, which saw hundreds of Hurons wasting away to the disease. The blame, perhaps understandably, was placed upon the European Jesuits. After an exceptionally horrendous epidemic in 1639, enraged Hurons began to vandalize and destroy chapels and schools, hoping to drive the Jesuits out of town.

Jean de Brébeuf

By 1641, 15 years after Brébeuf's arrival, the Jesuits had only managed to convert no more than 60 Hurons. Jesuits could tell that the Hurons were clearly still aggravated by the their presence and began to leave town, but Brébeuf opted to stay. In March of 1649, he was captured by a group of Iroquois rebels. Brébeuf, battered senseless and bound to a stake, had his limbs lopped off, his nails ripped off, and his tongue severed. It was said that his captors later tore out his heart and consumed his blood. Brébeuf's story soon leaked out into the public, allegedly prompting the conversion of at least 3,000 indigenous Canadians.

A more recent example is the story of the Miguel Pro, a Mexican Jesuit who lived during the oppressive Mexican Revolution. At the start of the revolution, 20-year-old Miguel was exiled due to the authority's violent persecution of the Catholics, and was only allowed to return home 15 years later. By then, he had already been formally ordained as a priest.

When Miguel returned to Mexico, all churches had shut down, and all the clergymen had gone underground. Those who were caught worshiping in public or in private, were taken out into the streets and mowed down by a firing squad. Even so, Miguel continued to run a clandestine ministry through coded messages and different disguises, posing as a beggar, a street sweeper, and even a policeman. With the help of his disguises, he carried out baptisms, confessions, marriages, and other sacramental rites.

Miguel was later falsely accused of a failed assassination attempt on President Plutarco Calles, and was double-crossed by a few of his former followers, who handed him over to the authorities. Plutarco immediately called for Miguel's execution. On that fateful day, Miguel dropped to his knees before the firing squad. He not only prayed, but forgave his executioners. It was said that Miguel refused the blindfold offered to him, and looked his killers square in the eye. As they cocked their guns, Miguel took his last breath and declared, "Long live Christ the king!"

Scandal

"The Jesuits...are a secret society – a sort of Masonic order – with superadded features, revolting odiousness, and a thousand times more dangerous." – Samuel Morse, American inventor and author

No legend is free from scandal, and with the Jesuits, it was no different.

The earliest record of Jesuit conspiracy theories is found in the 17th-century pamphlet, Monita Secreta, also known as the "Secret Instructions of the Society of Jesus." This was a fabricated compilation of instructions which were said to have been designed by Claudio Acquaviva, the fifth Superior General of the order, known by others as the second founding father of the society. The pamphlet consisted of a brief history of the Jesuits, as well as a set of "unpublished" guidelines that outlined the Jesuits' rise to power, often through underhanded and illegal methods.

An excerpt from the preface of a translated version of the pamphlet reads, "They were not allowed to be made known even to many members of a certain class of Jesuits. They had bold, daring bad men to achieve desperate deeds, and take off their enemies by steel or bullet, or poisoned chalice...They also had disguised agents, men in mask...They had shrewd, crafty, courteous, and most polished men, who courted nobles, insinuated themselves into the favor of princes, kings, rich widows, and young heirs and heiresses..."

More conspiracy theories surfaced during the Enlightenment era, exacerbated by the powerful waves of anti-Catholic sentiment in Europe. Historians such as the French anticlerical conservatives, Edward Quinet and Jules Michelet, were some of the first to declare an intellectual "war with the Jesuits." Another French novelist portrayed the order as a "secret society bent on world domination by all available means."

An entire genre of conspiracy theories would be written in the following centuries, accusing reviled historical leaders and tyrants of being part of the evil Jesuit agenda.

Anti-Jesuit conspiracy theories were once used as a propaganda tool by the Nazis during World War II. One of these works was the infamous pamphlet, "The Jesuit: The Obscurantist Without a Homeland," which discussed the Jesuits' "mysterious intentions," and how they harbored "dark powers." With that in mind, conspiracy theorists claim Hitler's hatred of the Jesuits was nothing but a facade. Hitler, although known for once referring to the Jesuits as "public vermin," supposedly had this to say to one of his associates before his rise: "I learned much from the Order of the Jesuits. Until now, there has never been anything this grandiose, on the earth, than hierarchical organization of the Catholic Church. I transferred much of this organization into my own party... I am founding an order... In my 'Burgs' of the Order, we will raise up a youth which will make the world tremble..."

Some say that Hitler's fixation on eliminating the Jews was the product of decades of Jesuit brainwashing, as the order wanted to prevent the Jews from controlling Israel. Other theorists disagree. Apparently, the Jesuits wanted Hitler to deliver the Jews to Palestine, where they would clash with the Arabs. The pope would then intervene, put a stop to these wars, and emerge as a hero, which would turn the church's damaged reputation around. One more theory suggests that World War II was the Jesuits' long-awaited revenge on Japan, who had banned the order from their nation back in the 16th century.

Another rumored Jesuit agent was Fidel Castro, a man that some armchair theorists have labeled a veteran "Jesuit puppet." Castro, who was a troubled student, would switch schools multiple times before landing in the Jesuits' care. He soon became the loyal pupil of a 24-year-old Jesuit novice who would mold him into the man he would one day be. This same novice was said to have foretold Castro's destiny, once scrawling the following message across the future dictator's yearbook: "Fidel Castro has the makings of a hero, the history of his motherland will have to speak about him."

When Castro graduated from law school, he joined the Orthodox Democrat Party, which some claim were stealthily run by the Roman Catholics. The Latin American Jesuits began to adopt Marxist-Leninist theology and became "fanatic left-wing Communists." These were principles Castro would later rigorously push for on behalf of the order. Of course, it is important to remember that the majority of these theories were concocted by Alberto Rivera, a notorious anti-Catholic activist.

Then, there was Jim Jones, founder of the People's Temple cult, yet another alleged Jesuit disciple. Some insist that the Jonestown Massacre, which saw more than 900 of its members commit mass suicide through the consumption of poisoned Kool-Aid, had been a plot conceived by the Jesuits and the Catholic Church. "Evidence" can be found in Jones' undisclosed relationships with a number of high-ranking figures, both political and religious. One of Jones' associates was said to have been Father M. J. Divine. Divine was a "gifted" preacher who called himself the "Second Coming of the Christ," and often claimed to receive regular visions from the heavens. Jones later met with suspected Jesuits, First Lady Rosalynn Carter and the California governor, Jerry Brown, to raise awareness about his movement. All 3, among a few others, purportedly knew about the mass suicide beforehand, but refused to sound the alarm bells.

The order's thirst for power saw no limits. According to another legend, J. P. Morgan, the Rockefellers, and the Rothschilds were summoned to a secret gathering by the Jesuits in 1910 to discuss the creation of the Federal Reserve Bank. This, which would become the central banking system of the United States, would be the order's gateway to achieving total authority over the world economy. The Jesuits listed Isador Strauss, John Astor, and Benjamin Guggenheim, 3 of the wealthiest men in the world, as potential disruptions to their scheme. And so, these men would have to be killed. The Jesuits knew that putting a hit on any of these men would have been too risky of a solution, so J. P. Morgan, the owner of White Star Lines, was commissioned to build the RMS Titanic. All 3 men were invited on board, and the rest is history.

Perhaps one of the most absurd of all these Jesuit-related theories is the "Black Pope Conspiracy." Black popes are the real operators of the Catholic Church who lurked behind the scenes, while "white popes," who are revealed to the public, are merely fronts. These black popes are said to have orchestrated some of the world's worst economical meltdowns and terrorist attacks, such as 9/11. Once again, Alberto Rivera is one of the main sources of these accusations. One such evidence is Rivera's claim of having once attended a "Black Mass" in Spain in the 1960s, which was held in honor of

Lucifer.

This would only be one of the order's many supposed ties to the dark side. The conspiracy website, Reptilian Dimension, claims that the order has since branched out into demonic cults, one example being the "Jesuit Ninth Circle." In the 2010s, Canadian authorities raided a series of satanic cults. Investigators recovered evidence of dark worship, such as videos of tortured children, as well as altars and books soaked in human and animal blood. Witnesses later testified that children had been dragged into underground satanic temples and sacrificed at the altar. Among the present during these rituals were the Jesuit Superior General and the "White Pope."

Despite the fact that these ludicrous stories have, for the most part, been disproven on multiple occasions, conspiracy theories continue to pour in to the archives of the boundless internet. Then again, perhaps that is the unavoidable consequence of creating such a formidable legacy. On October 24, 2016, Arturo Sosa was elected the Society of Jesus' 31st Superior General. Today, the order continues to be the largest male religious order of the Catholic Church, with a membership of over 16,000 priests, lawyers, doctors, teachers, and scholastics around the world. And perhaps even more notably, in March of 2013, Jesuits once again made history when Pope Francis rose to the papal throne, becoming the world's first ever Jesuit pope.

Online Resources

Other books about Catholic history by Charles River Editors

Other books about medieval history by Charles River Editors

Other books about the Jesuits on Amazon

Bibliography

1. Trueman, C. N. "The Jesuits." *The History Learning Site*. The History Learning Site, Ltd., 17 Mar. 2015. Web. 23 Jan. 2017.

<http://www.historylearningsite.co.uk/the-counter-reformation/the-jesuits/>.

2. Gascoigne, Bamber. "HISTORY OF THE JESUITS." *History World.* History World, Ltd., 2001. Web. 23 Jan. 2017. <http://www.historyworld.net/wrldhis/PlainTextHistories.asp?ParagraphID=hrk>.

3. Linton, Caroline. "Pope Francis Is a Jesuit: Seven Things You Need to Know About the Society of Jesus." *The Daily Beast.* The Daily Beast Company, LLC, 14 Mar. 2013. Web. 23 Jan. 2017. <http://www.thedailybeast.com/articles/2013/03/14/pope-francis-is-a-jesuit-seven-things-you-need-to-know-about-the-society-of-jesus.html>.

4. Trueman, C. N. "The Roman Catholic Church in 1500." *The History Learning Site.* The History Learning Site, Ltd., 20 Oct. 2016. Web. 23 Jan. 2017. <http://www.historylearningsite.co.uk/the-counter-reformation/the-roman-catholic-church-in-1500/>.

5. Moore, Nolan. "10 Crazy Catholic Conspiracy Theories." *Listverse.* Listverse, Ltd., 21 Aug. 2013. Web. 23 Jan. 2017. <http://listverse.com/2013/08/21/10-crazy-catholic-conspiracy-theories/>.

6. Individual, The. "The Jesuit Order Exposed." *Reptilian Dimension.* WordPress, 8 June 2014. Web. 23 Jan. 2017. <https://reptiliandimension.wordpress.com/2014/06/08/the-jesuit-order-exposed-2/>.

7. Knight, Kevin. "The Society of Jesus." *New Advent.* The Immaculate Heart of Mary, 15 Aug. 2016. Web. 23 Jan. 2017. <http://www.newadvent.org/cathen/14081a.htm>.

8. Editors, Got Questions. "What is the Society of Jesus? Who are the

Jesuits, and what do they believe?" *Got Questions.Org.* Got Questions Ministries, 2017. Web. 23 Jan. 2017. <https://www.gotquestions.org/Jesuits-Society-of-Jesus.html>.

9. Trueman, C. N. "The Medieval Church." *The History Learning Site.* The History Learning Site, Ltd., 5 Mar. 2015. Web. 23 Jan. 2017. <http://www.historylearningsite.co.uk/medieval-england/the-medieval-church/>.

10.   Editors, Protestant Reformation. "The Sale of Indulgences." *Protestant Reformation.* Weebly, 2011. Web. 23 Jan. 2017. <http://protestantreformationnhd.weebly.com/sale-of-indulgences.html>.

11.   Editors, PBS. "Counter-Reformation." *PBS.* Devillier Donegan Enterprises, 2014. Web. 23 Jan. 2017. <http://www.pbs.org/empires/medici/renaissance/counter.html>.

12.   Bovey, Alixe. "Death and the afterlife: how dying affected the living." *British Library.* British Library Board, 2014. Web. 23 Jan. 2017. <https://www.bl.uk/the-middle-ages/articles/death-and-the-afterlife-how-dying-affected-the-living>.

13.   Hays, Jeffrey. "CHRISTIANITY, HEAVEN AND HELL." *Facts and Details.* Jeffrey Hays, Mar. 2011. Web. 23 Jan. 2017. <http://factsanddetails.com/world/cat55/sub353/item1402.html>.

14.   Staff, Listverse. "Top 10 Legacies of the Middle Ages." *Listverse.* Listverse, Ltd., 19 Dec. 2009. Web. 23 Jan. 2017. <http://listverse.com/2009/12/19/top-10-legacies-of-the-middle-ages/>.

15.   Staff, British Library. "The three living and the three dead princes, from the 'De Lisle Psalter'" *British Library.* British Library Board, 2014. Web. 23 Jan. 2017. <https://www.bl.uk/collection-items/the-three-

living-and-the-three-dead-princes-from-the-de-lisle-psalter>.

16.   Graves, Dan, MSL. "Infamous Indulgence Led to Reformation." *Christianity.Com*. Salem Web Network, 2016. Web. 23 Jan. 2017. <http://www.christianity.com/church/church-history/timeline/1501-1600/infamous-indulgence-led-to-reformation-11629920.html>.

17.   Editors, History Channel. "Martin Luther Sparks a Revolution." *History Channel*. A&E Television Networks, LLC, 2015. Web. 23 Jan. 2017. <http://www.history.com/topics/martin-luther-and-the-95-theses>.

18.   Roccasalvo, Joan L., CSJ. "St. Ignatius of Loyola and his letters to women." *Catholic News Agency*. CNA, 31 July 2012. Web. 23 Jan. 2017. <http://www.catholicnewsagency.com/column/st-ignatius-of-loyola-and-his-letters-to-women-2247/>.

19.   Staff, Ignatian Spirituality. "St. Ignatius Loyola." *Ignatian Spirituality*. Loyola Press, 2009. Web. 23 Jan. 2017. <http://www.ignatianspirituality.com/ignatian-voices/st-ignatius-loyola>.

20.   Editors, Catholic Online. "St. Ignatius Loyola." *Catholic Online*. Catholic Online, 2016. Web. 23 Jan. 2017. <http://www.catholic.org/saints/saint.php?saint_id=56>.

21.   Staff, TFP. "Saint Ignatius of Loyola Biography." *The Famous People*. The Famous People, Ltd., 2017. Web. 23 Jan. 2017. <http://www.thefamouspeople.com/profiles/saint-ignatius-of-loyola-1666.php>.

22.   Traub, George, SJ, and Debra Mooney, PhD. "A Biography of St. Ignatius Loyola (1491-1556): The Founder of the Jesuits." *Xavier*

University. Xavier University Press, 2015. Web. 23 Jan. 2017.
<http://www.xavier.edu/mission-identity/heritage-tradition/who-was-St-Ignatius-Loyola.cfm>.

23.   Editors, St. Mary. "St. Ignatius of Loyola ." *St. Mary Magdalen Catholic Parish*. St. Mary Magdalen Catholic Parish, 2017. Web. 23 Jan. 2017.
<http://www.stmarymagdalen.org/Catholicism/Saints/StIgnatius.htm>.

24.   Rickard, J. "The Italian Wars, 1494-1559." *History of War*. History of War, 3 Oct. 2014. Web. 24 Jan. 2017.
<https://www.revolvy.com/main/index.php?s=Italian%20War%20of%201536%E2%80%931538&item_type=topic>.

25.   Zidkiyah. "Quotes About the Jesuit Order ("Society of Jesus") From Famous People." *Scribd*. Scribd, Inc., 2014. Web. 24 Jan. 2017.
<https://www.scribd.com/doc/30408550/Quotes-About-the-Jesuit-Order-From-Famous-People>.

26.   Staff, IMJC. "The Society of Jesus." *Immaculate Conception Jesuit Church*. Immaculate Conception Jesuit Church, 2015. Web. 24 Jan. 2017. <http://jesuitchurch.net/learn/the-society-of-jesus>.

27.   Knight, Kevin. "Ratio Studiorum." *New Advent*. The Immaculate Heart of Mary, 2014. Web. 24 Jan. 2017.
<http://www.newadvent.org/cathen/12654a.htm>.

28.   Staff, 867 Questions. "Was there ever a Woman Jesuit?" *867 Questions*. Blogspot, 17 Nov. 2005. Web. 24 Jan. 2017.
<http://867questions.blogspot.tw/2005/11/17-was-there-ever-woman-jesuit.html>.

29.   Staff, Times of Malta. "Ignatius of Loyola and the expansion of the Jesuit Order." *Times of Malta*. Times of Malta, Ltd., 20 Apr. 2014. Web.

24 Jan. 2017.
<http://www.timesofmalta.com/articles/view/20140420/life-features/Ignatius-of-Loyola-and-the-expansion-of-the-Jesuit-Order.515874>.

30.   Staff, Abagond. "Money in Leonardo's time." *Abagond*. WordPress, 10 May 2007. Web. 24 Jan. 2017. <https://abagond.wordpress.com/2007/05/10/money-in-leonardos-time/>.

31.   Staff, SOL. "SODALITY OF OUR LADY." *Sodality of Our Lady*. Sodality of Our Lady, 2016. Web. 24 Jan. 2017. <http://www.sodality.ie/index.php?option=com_content&view=article&id=21&Itemid=44>.

32.   Staff, New World Encyclopedia. "Chinese Rites Controversy." *New World Encylopedia*. MediaWiki, 15 May 2013. Web. 25 Jan. 2017. <http://www.newworldencyclopedia.org/entry/Chinese_Rites_Controversy>.

33.   Editors, Jesuits in Britain. "THE SUPPRESSION AND RESTORATION OF THE JESUITS." *Jesuits in Britain*. Jesuits in Britain, 2013. Web. 25 Jan. 2017. <http://www.jesuit.org.uk/suppression-and-restoration-jesuits>.

34.   Rao, John C., PhD. "The Venetian Interdict of 1606-1607." *Seattle Catholic*. Seattle Catholic, Ltd., 21 Sept. 2004. Web. 25 Jan. 2017. <http://www.seattlecatholic.com/article_20040921.html>.

35.   Staff, NNDB. "St. Ignatius of Loyola." *NNDB*. Soylent Communications, 2016. Web. 25 Jan. 2017. <http://www.nndb.com/people/626/000094344/>.

36.   Liotta, Paul. "The Pope's in America: 5 things you should know

about the order he belongs to ." *New York Daily News*. The Associated Press, 23 Sept. 2015. Web. 25 Jan. 2017. <http://www.nydailynews.com/news/national/5-jesuits-article-1.2371628>.

37.   Staff, Gettysburg. "CONVERSION TACTICS ." *Gettysburg Education*. The Gettysburg College, 2011. Web. 25 Jan. 2017. <http://public.gettysburg.edu/~tshannon/hist106web/Indian%20Convert s/Conversion%20Tactics.htm>.

38.   Editors, UCA News. "Why were the Jesuits suppressed?" *UCAN News*. UCAN News, Ltd., 30 July 2013. Web. 25 Jan. 2017. <http://www.ucanews.com/news/why-were-the-jesuits-suppressed/68845>.

39.   Kassebaum, Andrew. "Scientific Geniuses and Their Jesuit Collaborators." *Strange Notions*. Kickstart Media, Inc., 2015. Web. 25 Jan. 2017. <http://www.strangenotions.com/scientific-geniuses-and-their-jesuit-collaborators/>.

40.   Odenbach, Frederick, SJ. "Some Jesuits and Their Geophysical Observatories." *Fairfield University*. Fairfield University, 2005. Web. 25 Jan. 2017. <http://faculty.fairfield.edu/jmac/sj/geophysics.htm>.

41.   Kassebaum, Andrew. "How Catholic Missionaries Brought Science to China." *Strange Notions*. Kickstart Media, Inc., 2014. Web. 25 Jan. 2017. <http://www.strangenotions.com/how-catholic-missionaries-brought-science-to-china/>.

42.   Staff, TCR. "Jesuit Heroes Through the Years." *The Catholic Register*. The Shepherd's Trust, 2015. Web. 25 Jan. 2017. <http://www.catholicregister.org/jesuits-in-canada-list-sp-985240070/item/12960-jesuit-heroes-through-the-years>.

43.   Ghezzi, Bert. "Blessed Miguel Pro, SJ (1891-1927)." *Ignatian Spirituality*. Loyola Press, 2015. Web. 25 Jan. 2017. <http://www.ignatianspirituality.com/ignatian-voices/20th-century-ignatian-voices/blessed-miguel-pro-sj>.

44.   Staff, Catholic News Agency. "BLESSED MIGUEL PRO JUAREZ." *Catholic News Agency*. CNA, 23 Nov. 2016. Web. 25 Jan. 2017. <http://www.catholicnewsagency.com/saint.php?n=397>.

45.   Individual, The. "Jesuit Ninth Circle satanic cult." *Reptilian Dimension*. WordPress, 17 Sept. 2014. Web. 26 Jan. 2017. <https://reptiliandimension.wordpress.com/2014/09/17/jesuit-ninth-circle-satanic-cult/>.

46.   Brownlee, W. C., DD. "Secret Instructions of the Jesuits." *Masters Table*. The Collegiate Reformed Dutch Church, 2014. Web. 26 Jan. 2017. <http://www.masters-table.org/forinfo/wc-brownlee-secret-instructions-of-the-jesuits.pdf>.

47.   Staff, A Plane Truth. "Fidel Castro: Jesuit Puppet for 50 Years." *A Plane Truth*. WordPress, 27 Nov. 2016. Web. 26 Jan. 2017. <https://aplanetruth.info/2016/11/27/fidel-castro-jesuit-puppet-for-50-years/>.

48.   Staff, Spiritually Smart. "Jesuit Manipulated Catholic Nazis." *Spiritually Smart*. WordPress, 2011. Web. 26 Jan. 2017. <http://www.spirituallysmart.com/nazi.html>.

49.   Editors, JGC6. "Father Arturo Sosa SJ, 31st General of the Society of Jesus." *Jesuits General Congregation 36*. Society of Jesus, 14 Oct. 2016. Web. 26 Jan. 2017. <http://gc36.org/gc36-new-father-general/>.

50.   Woodbury, Sarah. "Life Expectancy in the Middle Ages." *Romance and Fantasy in Medieval Wales*. WordPress, 11 Mar. 2014. Web. 26

Jan. 2017. <http://www.sarahwoodbury.com/life-expectancy-in-the-middle-ages/>.

51.   Toth, Andrew L. *Missionary Practices and Spanish Steel: The Evolution of Apostolic Mission in the Context of New Spain Conquests.* N.p.: IUniverse, 2012. Print.

52.   Ross, Leslie D. *Medieval Art: A Topical Dictionary*. N.p.: Greenwood, 1996. Print.

53.   Sekules, Veronica. *Medieval Art* . N.p.: Oxford U Press, 2001. Print.

54.   Idigoras , J Ignacio Tellech, and Cornelius Michael Buckley. *Ignatius of Loyola: The Prigrim Saint*. N.p.: Loyola Press, 1994. Print.

55.   Gilbert, Josiah Hotchkiss, and Charles S. Robinson. *Dictionary Of Burning Words Of Brilliant Writers: A Cyclopaedia Of Quotations, From The Literature Of All Ages*. N.p.: Kessinger Publishing, LLC, 2009. Print.

56.   Loyola, Ignatius Of. *Letters of St. Ignatius of Loyola*. N.p.: Loyola Press, 1959. Print.

57.   Sarmento, Clara. *Women in the Portuguese Colonial Empire: The Theatre of Shadows*. N.p.: Cambridge Scholars Publishing, 2008. Print.

58.   Cushner, Nicholas P. *Why Have You Come Here?: The Jesuits and the First Evangelization of Native America*. N.p.: Oxford U Press, 2006. Print.

59.   Widdowson, Frederick. *A Bible Believer Looks At World History*. N.p.: Lulu.Com, 2011. Print.

60.   Higgins, Michael W., and Douglas Letson. *The Jesuit Mystique*.

N.p.: Loyola Press, 1995. Print.

61.   Burnett, Thom. *Conspiracy Encyclopedia: The Encyclopedia of Conspiracy Theories*. N.p.: Chamberlain Bros., 2005. Print.

Free Books by Charles River Editors

We have brand new titles available for free most days of the week. To see which of our titles are currently free, click on this link.

Discounted Books by Charles River Editors

We have titles at a discount price of just 99 cents everyday. To see which of our titles are currently 99 cents, click on this link.

Made in the USA
Monee, IL
16 February 2020